RON HOLLOWAY

HOW TO BE

LIGHT
SKIN

Printed in the United States of America

iamronholloway.com

ISBN-10: 0692744290
ISBN-13: 978-0692744291
Library of Congress Control Number: 2017964319

Edited by Nicole Lewis
Illustrations by Diego Hughes (pages 53, 55, 57, and 59)

All of us are 99% genetically alike. The only difference is our color pigmentation. To social intelligence, transcendentalism, comedy, love and respect.

"Oh, you a ol' light-skinned pretty motha @#$%!*"
- Tracy Morgan to Ron before the show at the Virginia Beach Funny Bone Comedy Club

RON HOLLOWAY

HOW TO BE

LIGHT
SKIN

CONTENTS

Introduction

After 30+ years, I've descended like Prince doing a reverse-dunk in Dave Chappell's skit to deliver the easy-to-use handbook on being light-skinned. "Game! Blouses!"

Seriously though, what, exactly, is light-skinned? How do you define it? Do you find yourself unable to understand or appreciate the light-skinned experience? Do you need help overcoming the labels – good, bad or other that are constantly placed on "light skins"? If that is true, then it doesn't matter if you're young or old, or black or white, in How to be Light-Skin, you will discover cause & effect, dos and don'ts, and actionable steps you can take to have a more fulfilling day-to-day experience, or a better understanding of the paper bag complexioned species.

We as a people are always consciously or subconsciously concerned about complexion. Kendrick Lamar would say, "It don't mean a thang." But it does — transcending race, advertisement, and social acceptability. According to Outliners author Malcolm Gladwell (a light-skin), it takes 10,000 hours to reach mastery; that means you're in great hands. After 34 years, this book has evolved to give you the cheat code and cliff notes to a piece of the complexion experience.

Each section of this guide contains amazing stories, tips, and common sense approaches to assist you with complex light-skinned-ness issues. With new insight and tactical advantage, you'll be way ahead of the crowd saying, "Oh, I know why that light-skin did that." People will call you fascinating and insightful. You will be respected for said knowledge. You'll have better relationships with people and parties will seem a lot more fun. You made the first step by caring enough to pick up this book. So turn the page and let a sample of the color wheel begin!

.

Working Hard? Or is Your Light-Skin Working?

Long, long ago in a distant land I had my first corporate job. I was on the job for probably about a month or two when one day my manager turns to me and says, "You know people say I only hired you for your looks, right?" I was pissed — like WTF, am I just "passing" here or something? They acquired me using the "paper bag test"? In my mind I'm thinking that anybody who has ever known me knows I am, and always have been, a hard worker. So, all this time at this company I busted my butt, only to be viewed as a "trophy piece." But, honestly, I fell into a deep, blacked out haze (no pun intended) reminiscing. I thought of all the times I heard people say of others, "He only got that job, title or role because he was light-skinned." Now they were putting that label on me.

You see – whether true or not – there are myths that exist about opportunity and being light-skinned. One such myth means you are more apropos to receive better employment opportunities than darker-skinned contemporaries. In fact, and according to BougieBlackGirl.com, a 2006 University of Georgia study lay claims to this phenomenon by concluding employers preferred light-skinned black men to dark-skinned men, regardless of qualifications.

Therefore, it is imperative as a light-skin you exemplify hard work. Potentially through no fault of your own, you bear a heavy responsibility. It's part of your light-skin inheritance... like rose petals on the ground in Coming to America.

Whether you want it or not, this responsibility was laid at the feet of light-skins long ago. It continues to even now, and in my opinion, for perpetuity like a ripple in an infinity pond.

Here is how it all started:

At around age 14 or 15, I made a routine trip to my best friend Kelvin's house on the other side of town. I caught the bus over there so we could get into our normal routine – video games, checking on girls, and going to his local basketball court to hoop. When I got in the door, Mr. Love (Kelvin's father's last name and what I always called him) ordered us to the kitchen table. He said, "Sit down gentlemen. I want to talk to you." Stomach nerves, bubble guts, and a slight fright came over me; anxious and thinking, "Aww damn! What did we do now?" Kelvin and I share an uncanny mental telepathy so to calm our nerves, we both instinctively reached into the kitchen fridge and pantry, which was only steps away, to grab some chips, soda and chocolate chip breakfast bars.

Now all seated, Mr. Love pulled out a thin, visibly very used book. The cover was barely readable. The book looked like it had been under the seat cushion of a couch that people had sat on for years unaware of its presence. I looked at the chaffed book while still dazed and confused. Poker face, he tossed it closer to us as we sat opposite of him at the table. I picked the book up first and quietly read the title aloud, "The Letters of Willie Lynch." I remember reading the subtitle to myself aloud in my mind, but my lips moved as I read along with no sound coming out.

This book was a "how-to" for other slave owners in the American South and everywhere else as you might imagine. I was shocked. Was this some joke? Mr. Love was cool, but he definitely wasn't "friend dad" – the father who is always trying to be his child's BFF. Yet, now that I knew what I had in front of me, and still confused about Mr. Loves' motives, he said, "You two will sit there and read this book before you continue on to anything else." The book wasn't a particularly long book, so we began to read. The elements of the day shifted. Daylight ended and light turned to dark outside. The more I read, my emotions shifted from boredom to intrigued to pain to anger.

Like the two elements of day – dark and light – one chapter put my thinking and perspective of the two to the test. In one of the chapters, Willie Lynch explains the methodology of his divide and conquer strategy to manage the Negro slave. Lynch would intentionally and purposefully separate the light Negro workers from the darker Negro workers. He would intentionally put those of darker hues in the field to do the arduous, hard manual labor while keeping those of the lighter complexion in the house to do less tenuous duties and to reap all the comforts of being inside the home like readily available water, cooler temperatures, etc. Right now are you wondering why? Well, Willie Lynch instructed that by creating this segregated working environment or colored caste system for the slaves, darker skinned slaves will become envious of those slaves with lighter complexions. Next, confrontation and infighting between the two will ensue which is a form of conflicting tribalism. Lynch explained you benefit as a slave owner because if they are divided and against each other, then they will not become, nor forge, a united front against you as the slave owner. Willie Lynch theorized this form of internal conflict and hatred will psychologically promulgate for all time, which means they will never be able to be a united people.

My friend Kelvin and I were equally shocked. The next few chapters were a blur and only turned the vice tighter on my brain. Yet, as a light-skin, that aforementioned chapter stuck with me amongst the rest. By the time we finished reading the book, our sodas, which were barely sipped, were flat, our potato chips didn't taste right, perhaps stale is a better word, and the chocolate chips in our breakfast bars melted. With the WTF look on our faces, my friend Kelvin and I closed the book and slowly shoved it back to Mr. Love – as if we were passing a secret note in class that we didn't want the teacher to confiscate or see. Mr. Love looked at us and said, "You won't find that in the bookstore. But it exists and most people don't know it exists." After we were done Mr. Love offered no Bible study, follow-up questions, or "what did you learn." He got up and walked upstairs and away. In some form of weird unspoken psychology, he wanted us to internalize what we had just read for ourselves. It felt like I was asking myself a hoard of closed-ended questions, but questions that had no voices or answers.

Dude definitely ruined my day. But he changed my thinking and my reality. It was like before that day my mind was a house filled with smoke, only now a window opened, and in came the fresh air.

But enough about me. This is about you, light-skin. What should you do with what you've just learned? First, don't be a square; be aware. Because there are huge numbers of light-skins out there that are oblivious to these underpinnings. Or worse yet, they just don't care. There is nothing worse than a light-skin with no emotional intelligence. So remember... just being self-aware is more than enough. As you engage in opportunities, assume the negative. Am I working my best and hardest relative to others? Think to yourself- "If my complexion were different, would the opportunity be different"? Maybe you might remember the research study I mentioned earlier. Maybe if you cast commercials, select magazine covers, or direct television shows you make sure every image or casting call member selected doesn't pass the "paper bag test." Maybe if you're a hiring manager, you ensure your employment selection was based on merit and skill, not just someone who more closely resembles your neighbors. Or, even better, maybe next time you follow someone who is dark-skinned or like his/her page on social media you do so genuinely, and not because they can sing, dance, run or jump really well.

Jokes (cough) aside, heavy is the knowledge. Heavy is the adopted burden. Therefore, as a light-skin, you must be confronted with that fact that this paradigm exists. What's more, although you haven't created the stereotypes, colorism, and discrimination, you must be aware of it. You must understand there will be no refund on the down payment for this particular innate cognition which others will undoubtedly have. But like my favorite Saturday morning cartoon used to say, "Knowing is half the battle."

Know Some History

The Problem

Somehow I was type casted as ignorant by a few, but more knowledgeable than many. You see, there's nothing like conferences to find a majority of people with whom one can share a love of intellectual interaction. Considering what I do, conferences are simply par for the course. On a gorgeous, clear and calm weekend, I attended one such conference.

After one of the laundry list of sessions I already attended ended, the conference agenda noted a scheduled break where nothing was really going on in preparation for dinner. So I moseyed on over to the bar, where I noticed other conference attendees and familiar faces sitting at the high-top bar tables observing happy hour. But they didn't notice me; their faces were focused like a drug dog looking for validation and were transfixed to the television.

They were learning, as I was about to, that while we were at this conference in Virginia – merely miles away – there was a break-out of fires, looting and vandalism in the city of Baltimore, Maryland. The collective action of events was sparked by the death of Freddie Gray, a young black male who died from injuries suffered while in police custody. All the major news networks had wall-to-wall coverage. On the television, I saw images of anger, confusion, and sadness on people's faces. In others images, I saw faces covered with masks and bandanas running with everything from sneaker boxes to two-ply toilet paper in their hands. I was unable to take my eyes away from the train wreck. The images also included cars being overturned, windows being shattered and massive mobs shouting and yelling. The undisputed highlight – for a lack of better words – was a scene that caught a mother running her son down in the chaos and repeatedly slapping him on the head for contributing to the riots.

After the shock wore off, there were around eight of us sitting and watching as a group from the high-top tables, the discussion shifted to race.

An observer from the group brought up racial profiling, stop and frisk policies and how quite often Black and Latino men are viewed as aggressive. In these settings, however, I know as a light-skin it's usually a good idea to pause, sit back and observe cautiously. I like to weed out the ignorant individuals by the comments they make – a fool will let you know they're a fool when they open their mouth sort of thing. Anyway, sure enough, as soon as I began to comment and share my thoughts concerning the subject, an individual at the table in a sly, jokingly remark says, "What do you know light-skin?" In his defense, however, I am pretty light-skin. I am quite often confused for being Spanish, or mixed with some form of Asian because of my small almond shaped eyes. But I smiled at his comment. Others smiled and laughed, too. A few did so uncomfortably. It was all-good — I grew up accustomed to those remarks whether they were directed at me seriously or not. Oh...and to my point... famous light-skinned people aren't immune to this problem either. Rain Pryor, a bi-racial light-skin and daughter of famed comedian Richard Pryor, in an interview with NBC NEWS said, "As I got older and in school, I was more upset in having to deal with black people, being light-skinned, than I had been with white people or any other ethnicity." Unfortunately for her, me, and you that's a problem. What's the antidote to the problem? You must know some history.

Knowing some history is critical for us. As a light-skin, you must know some history of your racial make-up. If, as a light-skin, you lack general cursory knowledge of your racial make-up you may find yourself in ostracized in some situations. Folks will assume you don't identify the way you say you do. Or more simply, that your ethnic make-up is not important to you. As I alluded to earlier, you will hear, "You're light-skinned! You don't know what it means to be Black (or fill in the ethnic blank)!" What that person is really saying is that you don't really belong to our tribe. You have been labeled a non-member and therefore unworthy of appreciating the rights, hopes and concerns of the race or ethnicity of which you identify with. People will assume you play whatever card is convenient and you're not "real." A life filled with and fueled by this conflicting identity issue can be very harmful to light-skins – in some cases likening it to a lifetime of being slowly deprived of oxygen.

The Cause
There's a subconscious convenient psychosis (yes, I meant to use that word) that exists regarding the light-skin and dark-skin experience. Somehow, if you're light, you're immune to institutional racism or not as nearly affected by it. There's somehow an absurd exaggeration that being lightly complexed means one cannot fully appreciate his or her ethnic experience. There somehow appears to be an

unwritten lineage that the lighter you are, the less "real" you must be. Is the above caused by self-inflicted socialization? Or is it perhaps, and most likely coming from misplaced values, attitudes and beliefs? Has much of this somehow become ignorant marching orders or normative directives? And yet, correlation does not imply causation. However, that doesn't mean emotions from these phenomena does not range from laughable to anger – see psychosis. See how I wrapped that up.

The Solution

Meanwhile, back in reality, don't be too light-skinned to care. No matter how you identify, or whatever insurmountable circumstances you face, know some history. Because it's not a matter if you'll be challenged on the history and culture of how you identify, but when you'll be challenged. And trust me! Nothing is more gratifying then when you know your history more than the person(s) challenging you. Their facial non-verbals are 100% guaranteed (with a gold star sticker) priceless.

To be light-skinned, you don't have to be a scholar on all ethnic topics, but you have got to know a little something-something. Feel me? Do some research. You don't need to be the Neil deGrasse Tyson of all things Black, Latino, and Asian. But you can't be "boo-boo the fool" or a "dun-da-dun" either. If you're Black, you should know the basic tenets of slavery and how Blacks got here. You should know the "Willie Lynch Theories." You should know the Civil Rights Movement of the '60s and the basic philosophies of civil rights leaders like Dr. Martin Luther King, Jr. You should be able to identify icons of the movement and match them with snippets of their bios. You should be somewhat versed and/ or well-read on the crack cocaine epidemic, racial profiling, and the prison industrial complex, just to name a few.

If you're Latin, you should know many of the same sentiments above. You should know aspects that stem from Latin history and/or affect Latin culture. For example, you should know the Treaty of Guadalupe Hidalgo, have a basic understanding of U.S. immigration policy, migrant worker issues, the "drug war" and the cause & effect it has had on many Central and South American countries.

The Wrap-Up

All your boy is saying here is – for example – if someone asked you who was Rosa Parks you should know she was tired, her feet probably hurt, and she stayed the hell in her seat. Somebody got mad… the rest is history. So help me help you, light-skin. You don't want somebody to ask you about the Emancipation Proclamation and you ask, "How do you do that dance?" Or if you see someone with a Jackie Robinson Brooklyn Dodgers jersey, you don't ask if L.A. just signed a new player?

Besides, speaking of "playas", remember that brother that assumed I was too light-skinned to "get it" in my story earlier? Do you also remember those guaranteed priceless facial expressions I mentioned earlier? All because I knew some history that night in question, whenever I spoke on any topic germane to the subject, he visibly looked as if he just licked an ashtray. Wrinkles covered his face, which, in this instance, symbolize surprise, respect, and cautious trust. Finally, his head would nod up and down slowly twice and very brief, almost unrecognizable to the naked eye –

signifying validation. And there you have it; valid is as valid does. Now isn't that what being light-skinned is really all about?

Be Super Humble

Do you feel useless when they say, "I don't date light-skins. They're too cocky"?

Have you been diagnosed as conceited? Symptoms include, "You think you're all that!" Or maybe people simply hate on you for no apparent reason and play down your accomplishments to others? If you suffer from the aforementioned ailments your light-skin locomotion can become highly unpredictable. The noise aside, if you want to learn how to be humble and never be given those labels in the first place, then this chapter has the prescription for you.

First, what does it mean to be humble? By definition it means having or showing a modest or low estimate of one's own importance. Take that definition literally. Allow it to merge with your light-skin heart strings. Because the only way you will meet the criteria of truly being humble is if your actions genuinely come from the heart. Let me give you my top three ways to get started.

1. Avoid Bragging

Let's start off with a major light-skin action you can take to increase your humble swag. Avoid bragging. Hold up. Let me circle back. Avoid bragging and humble bragging. Light-skins can be quite sneaky with the humble brag, too. And by humble-bragging I mean, "Yeah, I didn't do a lot this weekend. I just bought a new Benz and did some shopping. That's it really." And then you're like, "Wow, that was sneak-bragging to me on the low though."

Here's an example you're potentially sliding on the humble scale. If you're in a social setting with friends or new people you should hear the words, "Well, I... or I'm doing/did" no more than three or four times. Any more than that tips the scales towards narcissism or sociopath – it's hard distinguishing the two sometimes. No, seriously, it is. Instead, however, be a considerate light-skin in your conversations. Generally, ask questions that start with "tell me more about" ...; "how was that experience" or "how is your family doing?" Asking questions and follow-up questions is a practical way to avoid bragging. Avoiding bragging and being considerate goes super far in the light-skin brand, not to mention it's better for society. Research shows that at major companies and organizations employees appreciate other employees that are great listeners and ask questions the most. It shows you actually give a damn about what they're saying, and you're not just waiting on your turn to talk. Sound familiar?

And even talking is turning into a lost art. Am I right? Nowadays, people digitally download everything from food to conversations. So for those of you that prefer to digitally download yourself more, and talk less, I have tips for refraining from bragging. Let me give you some images to think about. Have you seen the pictures posted of designer bags, lavish trips and "the look who I'm with?" But, that's all a light-skin ever posts. Put this book down and check your social media right now to see if you fit the bill. If so, don't do that, okay. As a light-skin, you look especially bad and it screams insecurity and self-importance, which are character flaws you don't want to be aligned with. Humble is the word, remember? Now, and before I get you down, let me add one thing: I'm not a professor of buzz kill, or a member of the FOFP – Fraternal Order of Fun Police. So, yes – post away light-skins, but moderation is key. "Too much of anything can kill." Look up Plato's Allegory of the Cave, too much self-glorification will kill any semblance of humanity you very well may have. You can be happy to do nice things. You can be happy to have nice things. You just have to ask yourself: do I want to be known for collecting people and solid relationships? Or do I want to be known for collecting superficial relationships and things?

2. Help Others & Give Back

Embracing people leads to my next point for light-skin humbleness. To be light-skinned you must focus your energy on helping others. It should fall somewhere on your Maslow's hierarchy of needs. Why? Again, to alleviate those poor aforementioned labels and tags. Labels have consequences. Helping others, volunteering and giving back vastly changes that paradigm from which others view you. Others will have a more positive perception of you; they'll say, "Oh, look, she's a good light-skin." Steps you can take include mentoring kids or working with a disenfranchised group, donating time or money to a cause you're passionate about, or getting involved with anything other than yourself. Nothing screams humble more than engaging in one of those options. They pull at the people you know and don't know heartstrings. Be genuine though, because both the people who you want to like you and the people you're aiming to help will know if you are or not.

You shouldn't only give back or help others when a camera

crew is present or to post online. I had a light skinned acquaintance once who was so caught up in taking selfie pictures at a charity event just so he could look good on social media. True story. People of that sort make me sick. I'm a light-skin OG when it comes to this helping others and giving back thing; I've incorporated as a piece of my lifestyle.

Speaking of OGs, John Legend is a successful light-skin who exemplifies good intentions. I mention him because some light-skins can't do anything until they see others doing it first. So take Mr. Legend. If you Google looktothestars.org, you will see he has a laundry list of charities and causes he supports. I actually briefly shook his hand and gave him my admonishment in Phoenix, AZ in 2012. He was the keynote at the conference I was attending and spoke about the importance of education. You could see his genuine passion for service and scholarship, which is why his light-skinned success is not a surprise.

3. Deflection = Humility
How you as a light-skin handle fame, success, and recognition is vital to being humble. For example, think about all the successful stars you really admire. Now think about the successful stars ridiculed in the media daily? Are they two different sets of people? I'm guessing your answer is yes. Of course you like the celebrities who have more than an ounce of humility, whereas, the me-first stars are always in the news being lambasted for some arrogant action they took.

It works the same all throughout society.

Check out Russell Wilson. Have you noticed how the media and America are infatuated with him? Have you noticed if you sit in front of the TV for an hour, you may see Russell Wilson three or four times? Here's why. First, they love him because he's a winner. But, second, and more importantly, they love him because he never takes all the credit for his or the team's success, which is a trait of humility. How does this apply to you? Well, whether you came up with a sick 16 bars or created a dope excel sheet for your business team, don't take all the credit. Deflect some praise. Play it down. Give credit to the producers or Janice in accounting. You will watch people warm up to you quicker than a British boy band.

Cherish these humble carats. They're low hanging fruit filled with good light-skinned fibers for keeping you "regular." Think courtesy flush. Being a humble light-skin honestly costs you nothing, but you have a hell of a lot to gain, such as respect, friends, and gratitude. I'll end with this – the word humble has a "u"and "me". Focus more on the "u" in the world and less on the "me."

A Little Too Cute?

As a young kid on a bright sunny day, I loved nothing more than to ride around on my life-like child-sized toy motorcycle. One day while circling my house with my baby chopper on the sidewalk, my next door neighbor, a lady who was an antagonist and had repeated feuds with my mother, said to me, "You're too pretty to be your mother's son." Bad, bad move lady. My mother overheard her, a scuffle ensued, and my mother nearly bit half of my neighbor's face off. From there, I learned early on, and as I'll explain here, why being too cute is a problem for various reasons. You'll learn in this chapter why you need to stop always trying to be cute.

I'm sure you've heard the various call signs like "pretty Ricky," redbone, and exotic. These are all terms of endearment, right? Nope. If as a light-skin, you enjoy those labels then you're being too light-skin; that adjective (too) is meant to have a negative connotation by the way.

If you're way too concerned and/or consumed with looking cute, people will naturally be convinced you are simply shallow and vain. For instance, why does it take you 45 minutes to get ready for a 10-minute trip to the grocery store and back? Why are you more focused with the right matching shoes to your outfit than having a good time? How many times have you jeopardized having a great experience because your hair wasn't cut or perfectly styled? Sounds to me like the person being described above is the other light-skin; whereas, you want to be light-skin. Trust me, people will take notice, give you labels I mentioned earlier, and frame your presence in a box with a self-absorbed bowtie. And, honestly, you can't be mad if you fit the profile. Why? Well, Socrates said, "We are what we repeatedly do."

Here are a few tips to gain some grit while shedding the male metrosexual or the female bird tags. For starters, guys, leave the eyebrows alone. Enough already. One, your eyebrows make your facial expression look as if something is always on your mind – or like you want to say "good point" all the time. I'm constantly looking all around; you make my nerves bad. Light-skin dudes we can go a little further. Besides refraining from the cover girl eyebrows, maybe let your hair grow out and miss a line-up occasionally. Please don't dye your hair blonde! Also, some ladies go a little heavy making sure their face is perfect. Once in a while, just maybe, don't do the whole facial routine. What am I talking about? I'm talking about the the foundation, the concealer, the highlighter, the contouring and the pounds of make-up. I mean c'mon, that's an hour right there. Natural is cool sometimes.

Incorporating the points here into your daily routine will psychologically give people a more grounded perspective of you, light-skin. Don't believe me? I was in Atlanta, Georgia years ago with a friend. My friend's cousin, a local hip-hop artist, performed while I was down there. Long story short, we all hung out together, partying, clubbing, etc. After the second day, my friend's cousin turned to me at the bar and out of the blue said, "For a light-skinned dude you're pretty black." Funny, right? Who says that? But I knew immediately what he meant. He had been around me for a couple days and picked up on some of the nuances mentioned above.

I picked up a lot from playing in the sandbox as a kid. A visual learner, as a young light-skin, Redman was my example for making sure I wasn't being too cute. That's my dude and he's also a dope entertainer. Redman would do a TV show or rock a concert looking like he just woke up with sleep still in his eyes, hair crazy and all. But he was real. And definitely, definitely always had thought-provoking social commentary on life, hip-hop and the hood. Speaking of the hood, you may or not remember a TV show Redman did showcasing his "crib." To my point, when most entertainers did this show, their homes were in gated communities and were gluttonous, glamorous mansions; however, Redman had a super duper humble spot in the hood of Staten Island, NY. The show – totally searchable on the net – was straight hilarious! Straight classic! That's why you can understand why people would never say Redman was always trying to be cute, cocky or self-centered. You may not like the man, but appreciate the principle.

If principles are important to you and if you consider yourself a principled light-skin, then consider utilizing the tips here. Many light-skins will still have their own self-interest and deplete the collective good, making the rest of us suffer and look overly vain – see Tragedy of the Commons. For the few of you that are listening, you're not being asked to purposely look terrible. But, on GP (that's general purpose for novices) don't try to look perfect or cute all the light-skin time. Do you want to be considered more real? Do you want to be considered more genuine and less self-absorbed? Well, let your next move be your best move. Start now; this is a curable allergy - curable with natural remedies. It will leave you looking more natural and more real in the end.

Make Sure All Your Friends Aren't Light-Skin Too

Feet kicked up and sitting on the couch with an 11.2 fl. oz. in my hand, I had the tube on watching basketball. The Golden State Warriors were playing and I'm watching All-Star point guard Stephen Curry. During a break in the action, the sideline play-by-play commentators shift from talking about how "nasty" his game is on the court to a quick family profile of the All-Star point guard; they talked about how lovely and special Curry's family is. What pops up next on the screen, after one of Curry's on-court highlights, is the quintessential (front cover) catalog image of the perfect light-skinned family. I swear a saw an angelic glow emanate from my television screen and suddenly heard soft music playing in the background.

Even as a light-skin myself, I thought, "Man, if that was a clique that would be a whole lot of light-skin." Curry can't choose his family, but you can choose your friends. So, if your crew looks like the light-skinned starting five, then you're too light. It just sets me off as visibly awkward, like the person who only eats all cheese topping pizzas. Who does that? The problem optically comes across as tribal – the behavior or attitude that stems from a strong loyalty to one's own social group. Therefore, it makes you look uncomfortable making friends with people who don't resemble your appearance. Does that make sense?

On the basis of appearance, your brain is an intriguing organ. Here's why. According to a Harvard study published in the journal PLOS ONE, the first thing your brain does when it encounters people is take note of race and color. They found by studying the fusiform face area (FFA) that patterns of activation were different for black and white faces. The researchers, however, were uncertain of why exactly, but a reaction was observed nonetheless.

So what does it all mean?

Well, you may naturally or innately – albeit subconsciously – flock to the crayon that most resembles you in the box. Ask yourself this question though - who wants to color a coloring book with only one type of crayon? Ask a kid this question and watch his/her response. Make sure you have a video recorder handy, too. It just might go viral. The Q&A here is just like from my basketball story earlier; something just comes across as wrong. The cost for your homogenous image is perceived exclusion. Perception is reality, right? Because you know when folks see your pictures they will think, "Wow! She couldn't find one dark, caramel, hell, even white person to be in all those pictures." Next thing you know you're being labeled too light-skinned, along with being viewed as overly tribal. And, yes, remember – tribalism definitely covers skin colors, too. In case you didn't know tribalism is also Bloods vs. Crips, and Democrats vs. Republicans, and Hutu vs. Tutsi, and Shiite vs. Sunni just to add some color commentary (no pun intended).

But I digress.

It's your own life. You have your own light-skinned jurisdiction. Be a good, all-inclusive light-skin. One that is proud and stemming with colorful emotional intelligence. Remain self-aware. Are you only surrounding yourself with other light-skins? Are your social media friends and followers all similarly complexed? Check your social media posts and pictures right now. Do all the people in your crew look brighter than a 100-watt light bulb? Incandescent, too — I'm old school.

Besides, even in the old school Milli had no fun without Vanilli. Go get out there and add some flavor to your crew. Make sure all your friends aren't light-skinned too. A world where we're all the same is whack. One of my favorite comedians once said, "A world with all rich people would be incredibly boring." Better yet, think of it like ice cream. Would you only want to eat vanilla ice cream for the rest of your life? No other flavors? No fudge? No caramel? No nuts? No fruit toppings? Ever? Of course, you don't. Then, mix your entourage up and watch a cherry form on top.

Have to Have a Sense of Humor

Meet light-skinned Ricky. Light-skinned Ricky thought he was good; he thought he was the man around town. Ricky had all the trappings of the "in" and "it" crowd. Ricky had a dime for a girlfriend. Ricky had the freshest clothes. Ricky had a dripping s-curl. Ricky had talent. Ricky had what most people would consider material success. But, what Ricky didn't have was a sense of humor.

If you asked a group of people that knew Ricky to raise their hand and if they thought he was one of their favorite people, you might as well be asking who'd like to volunteer for jury duty. The results would be the same – slim to nil. Again, because Ricky had no sense of humor. Ricky took himself way too seriously and people didn't want to be around him. Other than his "things," he was persona non-grata. And as you may know, this form of alienation can be a common light-skin problem; although, many of us display an alternate façade. One of the many reasons for this alienation, however, is not being able to take a joke and others-on-self-deprecating humor.

What is not humorous, though, is the preconceived notion light-skins care more about personal looks and material possessions than anything else. For example, if you made a joke about Ricky's skinny jeans, he would get mad and hold a grudge. If you told Ricky his eyebrows were crooked, he'd get an attitude and want to fight. Ricky couldn't handle the small, light-hearted, and playful teasing. The dude wasn't being bullied or anything — it was just friends having fun in a social setting.

Right now you're thinking: "Ron, how come Ricky couldn't just 'do him'? What if I don't like being joked on and I just want to "do me?"

You see, light-skin, (gasp!) there's an inconvenient truth here. Open your mind wider for a second. Think about this: How rarely, often, or if ever, do you hear someone call a dark complexion individual a pretty boy or girl? Think hard... like all your life hard. I already know your answer. Now imagine how that phenomena influences the individual subconscious. Here's one way; having a lighter complexion is like being a woman. Hear me out. As an individual with lighter skin, if you don't smile often or don't appear to be as happy as a Pharrell Williams song all the time, then you must be the b-word, conceited, or moody. Ask a woman you know whether I'm lying or not. Ask women how many times they hear, "Oh, you should smile more sweetheart." But why? But what for? So it is a delicate dance and truth you must come to accept. Oddly, people think, "What?! You're light-skinned. You should always be happy and perky."

Now that we've got that out the way that you apparently can do no wrong, let's move on.

Ease on down the light-skin road. The wizard will tell you to start with small steps towards obtaining a sense of humor. Start by not taking yourself too seriously. If somebody jokes or criticizes you, join in with them – hell, even add-on by telling another self-deprecating joke and laugh along. Then the first thing that will come to their mind is wow, that person's cool. Or try this — when someone makes an ill-faded or negative comment about you – agree with it. I'll guarantee you that comment or critique will go away forever. Why? Because those types of individuals will no longer be able to get the emotional response from you they were looking for. 75% of the time, this works every time. In this example you'll win twice. One, by killing their wayward joy and two, appearing more personable and grounded.

By that logic, the more personable you appear, the more approachable you will appear to be as well. In our story, Ricky wasn't very personable or approachable. When you saw Ricky all you saw was perfect eyebrows, an s-curl, designer sneakers with designer jeans, and a male blouse. Ricky visibly had the emotions of a Secret Service agent with the posture to match; he didn't seem to enjoy anyone's company but his own. So the solution here is humor. Find the humor in life. Look for humor in people, places and things every day. Extend your hand to folks, break the ice, and try to make small talk more often. Unlike Ricky, you'll find people will gravitate towards you and genuinely enjoy being around you, which means you're now standing out for all the right reasons.

The right reasons also include health. Priceless, priceless health. I mentioned this point near the end because it is dumb important. As a light-skin you must maintain your health. Humor and laughing often is one way to accomplish this goal. Many studies, including those in medical journals, reveal both humor and laughter strengthens your immune system. It also reduces stress and stressful situations. If you follow, that's a primary objective of what how to be a light-skin is all about – less stress and better health.

Finally, while on your way to being a happier light-skin, remember to be cognizant. You may risk being characterized as too serious and lacking a sense of humor. Therefore, don't be like light-skin Ricky. Don't take yourself too seriously. Don't be constipated with your humor and emotions. I know it may hurt. I know it may be painful. But, who cares if they call you light bright? Who cares your s-curl doesn't curl just right? Who cares people think you're some other race? Embrace it. Smile about it. The price of being a better light-skin is going through those pains and getting stronger because of it.

Be Able to Fight

"You're light-skinned! Ain't nobody scared of you!"
- Somebody Funny

You've definitely heard of light-skins as being soft, "scaredy-cats" and not being able to fight. It is a well-known assumption played out in funny memes on social media, movies, and in real life. Trust me, if you're light-skinned you will be tested. Consequently, it's important you know how to "throw hands." You don't need heavyweight champion or knockout artist status, but you better have some moderately good fighting skills. Or at least be able to duck and ball-up well. You won't lose cool points; sometimes the best offense is a good defense.

Consider this: have you experienced a social scenario where, right or wrong, a person was attracted to you specifically because you were light? And somebody else in that scenario caught ill feelings towards you because of that fact. How about this example: you're playing basketball and destroying the person guarding you on the court - just making them look bad, not to mention the person guarding you has their significant other at the game. Next this bum who can't guard you calls you "light-bright" or the "color of piss." Okay, but enough about me.

On another more personal note, I remember stories from my mother detailing how the darker-skinned girls would bully her by saying things like she was too pretty to fight because she was light-skinned. My mother said the girls would tell her they were intentionally going for her face to "tear up that pretty little light-skin face." The light-skin hunger games my mother experienced created a social Darwinism within her. That's why for many of us, all of the above are reasons to be able to fight.

But why are light-skins considered soft? Where did it all start, Ron?

Well, think about it. For starters, think about the evolution and portrayal of Black action heroes in the media probably as far back as the 60s or 70s. You had Dolemite, Shaft, Action Jackson, Denzel and of course my personal favorite, Wesley Snipes (Passenger 57 was one of the greatest movies of all-time). Take a close look at these men. Do you notice what all these action heroes have in common? Not one looks like you! Therefore, there are no images of light-skins karate chopping, body slamming, or putting the hurt on three or four dudes in the media to create and condition that image. Maybe we need a minister of light-skin propaganda. Because there's "no there, there."

Instead, the light-skin images stew from slavery of which lights were in the house (chilling like life was sweet) looking soft, under fans, sipping cool water and tea. Meanwhile, the dark-skinned slaves were getting physical and in the fields going H.A.M. The image framing hasn't really changed but only now comes through a different visual medium. Lights are still portrayed as soft, gentle and non-threatening in media. You see it from Smokey Robinson to Al B. Sure, Prince and now Drake.

Since we've gone Hollywood here, let me give you some food for thought. You don't want to get beat-up, your chain snatched, and your bike taken like Red (a light-skinned) did by Debo in the movie Friday. "C'mon Debo! Stall em out! "What you got on my 40 oz., homie?" Red got caught in some bad light-skinned business. You must be in the business of letting folks know "you ain't gonna be no punk." If they mess with you there's going to be consequences and repercussions. No more will you be perceived as a soft-target.

Begin by targeting your inner-beast. You can do this by simply buying, renting or bootlegging the movie New Jack City. Why? Because the protagonists are two hard-hitting, thoroughly portrayed light-skin brothers. You have one as the deranged, badass uncontrollable cop. The other plays a tough-as-nails detective cop in the film. Unfortunately, however, they're going up against a dark-skin antagonist – always dividing us. Anyway, watch the flick three or four times. Watch the light-skins get busy. Study the tactics. Study the mannerisms. Embrace the swag. Recite the lines in the mirror. Look in the mirror and practice being tough. Don't let anybody mess with you. Don't let anybody say whatever they want to you. Have a spine. As a light-skin, you must reject the notion that you don't have a spin because of your non-confrontational nature.

Ah, but there's a caveat of course...

Please, please don't overcompensate. You know the light-skins that try to act extra hard to prove he/she is "built like that." They have to one-up your high-yellow realness.

Somehow only they can keep it light-skin 100 and they act as the light-skinned gatekeeper for realness. And they're usually harder on other light-skins they perceive as soft. I almost forgot — they will definitely do all this in front of dark-skinned counterparts to show-off and to be more accepted. Because somehow in their eyes darker skin equals more real. You know the symptoms; the diagnosis is insecurity. Please don't be that guy or gal. You know that as "lames" or "thugs-in-a-box". Overcompensating will only cause you more drama, stress, and unnecessary attention.

Who better to explain drama than Shakespeare who said, "All the world's a stage." Still that doesn't mean you have to be an actor. On occasion when you buy a product off the shelf, it's fine as seen on television; however, you may have to buy, create or customize additions to make the product work more efficiently, right?

Take control. You are your own product placement. Now you know when it comes to your physical prowess, history, television and music are unfortunately against you, light-skin. But when the chips are down and the light-skinned get tough, the light-skinned get going. Tighten up your bootstraps. Get yourself ready in those "butter Timbs." So what you're light-skinned and ain't nobody scared of you? Bob & weave. Learn to tuck and roll. Use your jab. These will prove valuable to becoming a complete light-skin. One day you'll be the reason Michael Ealy, secret British agent, stops a Russian crime boss by single-handedly infiltrating and destroying some secret evil empire - on screen no less. Can you picture that?

IF/THEN
LIGHT SKIN
SOBRIETY TEST

YOU MIGHT BE TOO LIGHT SKIN...

1. If you run to be in front of every picture, then you're being too light-skinned.
2. If all your pictures have duck lips, balled-up lips or sexy eyes, then you're being too light skinned.
3. If every time you get a haircut you post a side profile picture, then you're being too light-skinned.
4. If you tell people, "I got that good hair," then you're being too light-skinned.
5. If you're a light-skin and all you have ever date is other light-skins, then you're being too light-skinned.
6. If you wish you were light-skin, then you're being too light skinned.
7. If you're a light-skinned guy and you dye any part of your hair blonde, then you're being too light-skinned.
8. If you take a stupid amount of selfie pictures just to post one because none of the others were just right, then you're being too light-skinned.
9. If you are on the edge of being light-skinned, but closer to being dark-skinned and you swear to people, "I'm light-skinned," then you're being too light-skinned.

BONUS LIGHT SKIN TIPS

Bonus Light Skin Tip #1: Do not take too many side profile pictures if you are light-skinned. Nobody cares about your good hair, baby hairs or line-up. Stop always trying to be cute.

Bonus Light Skin Tip #2: Again, enough with all the sexy faces. Stop puckering up your lips and making sexy, smoky eye faces. You're doing the most and it looks ridiculous. You don't see Lisa Bonet, De Niro, or Denzel taking selfies.

Bonus Light Skin Tip #3: If you are light skin, take pictures of you hitting the punching bag, dunking (two hands) on somebody, participating in a mud-run, or something else that is rough and physical in nature.

Do take pictures to make it appear as if you're at least capable of "busting a grape in a fruit fight." This is important to the light-skin brand. Folks think light-skin = soft. There is a misnomer that we're mainly sweet as southern tea. And I like southern tea!

Bonus Light Skin Tip #4: Do take pictures of the good deeds you are doing in the community. This will help market the culture of volunteerism and philanthropy. That doesn't mean it has to be a selfie everytime. Mix it up and be creative. Perhaps take a picture of other people volunteering at the event. Light-skins are quite often perceived as self-centered. Helping others goes a long way and you'll feel better afterwards, even if it's not documented or if you don't get credit for it.

THE
LIGHT SKIN
APPEAL

Highest Level
Prince, Bruce Lee, Selena, Barack Obama, Harry Belafonte, MJ (2.0 light-skin version), Sade, Joan Baez, Cesar Chavez, Beyoncé...

Simply put, this group became symbols. They transcend all forms of racism and any color I.D. #officialbosses

Executive Suite

These spots are held for light-skin big names like Billie Holiday, J-Lo, Kim K., Drake, Kravitz, Pharrell, John Legend, Carlos Santana, and Jackie Chan. They are just about good anywhere and, are more than likely, recognized by the first or last name only status.

Note: Here are some questions the "masses" might ask before meritoriously advancing individuals into this group: Does he/she make me feel really comfortable (the masses LOVE when you make them feel "comfortable")? As a mom, can I see him/her dating my child? Can I picture them in a romantic comedy?

Mid-Grade
Common, J. Cole, Ariana Grande, Zoe Saldana, Bruno Mars, and Zendaya

Here, the optics of the light-skin brand matter; how much, we don't really know. These guys and gals definitely have "crossover" appeal. The group is mainstream and marketable.

Hurry-up and Buy
Malcolm X, Che Guevara, and Huey Lewis.

These individuals are legends in their own rights especially for their ability to galvanize large groups of people. However, it is said some people fear what they don't understand and hate what they cannot conquer. Therefore, making those in this range famous but persona non-grata in terms of ingratiating themselves with mass appeal.

LIGHT SKIN SCENARIOS

As a light-skin, you will find yourself in many life scenarios that will allow you to fully demonstrate how to be light-skin. Please see the next few exercises to see how you stack up.

SCENARIO #1: PRIME TIME

So your friend asks you and a group of friends to enter a contest in which this person is really excited about. The winning submission will get a five-minute infomercial during prime time of Super Bowl weekend.

Ultimately, and as luck would have it, your friend's entry is selected as the national winning submission. Turn up! Your friend is through the roof with excitement. One member of the winning team will be given a star role in the commercial. Your friend has always wanted to be on television and eagerly anticipates the star role in the infomercial.

But the situation is much, much more complex.

As the only light-skinned member in the group, the commercial director approaches you and says, "The role of the lead requires someone with a lighter complexion. We would like to cast you for that role. Are you interested?"

What should you do? (see next page for options)

SCENARIO #1: PRIME TIME CONT'D

All light-skinned things considered, which of the following statements best describes what you should do? Circle all that apply.

Answers:

A) Answer the director immediately, "Hell yeah!" and proceed accordingly without giving the situation any further thought or consideration.

B) Speak with the director, suggest your friend for the role, and explain to her/him that this means more to your friend than anything in the world.

C) Meet up with your friend and share the director's comments with that person. Then let your friend decide what you should do next.

D) Drop out of participating in the contest and commercial all together. You see no benefit to any of it.

SCENARIO #1: PRIME TIME CONT'D

If you answered B and C, then you're one step closer to being light-skinned on 100! Both B and C options show major light-skin consideration for your friend. The first choice (choice A) shows a complete lack of consideration for the environment or light-skinned situational awareness. In sniper school it's called ranging the light-skin zone. Choice B gives the director some perspective on the situation and the colorism from which his decision may have come. You're also setting up choice C. You now have to "chop it up" with your homie and because you two both love each other your friend will respect your honesty and openness. Thus, in the event the director doesn't change his/her mind, your friend will be less shocked and/or upset by the news. Option D is silly. If you are able, capable and have any inclination to do such an amazing thing, then you should. So stop acting like a big dummy. This opportunity might open doors for you, your family and your friends down the road.

.

SCENARIO #2: BRIGHT LIGHTS

You are headed out with your friends for a casual night out in the city. Once in the city, the group hits the bars and nightlife scene. After bar-hopping you end up at a very chill and classy establishment. Then all of the sudden one of your friends says, "Hey! Look over there. They're checking us out, too." As a group you casually make your way over slowly but surely. Now at the high-value targets, you say something smooth to one of them to break the ice and your friends slide right into position. The remainder of the night, and up until last call, you all chit chat and make small talk followed by everybody exchanging phone numbers.

Months later you find out through the grapevine someone in the group you approached from that special night out only dates light-skins and consequently likes you. But here's the dilemma: your best friend who is dark skinned fell in love at first sight with that person.

What do you do? (see next page for options)

SCENARIO #2: BRIGHT LIGHTS CONT'D

So what do you do in this situation? Do you:

A) Get with them anyway and let your friend find out by seeing you two together on social media

B) Sneak around and hope your friend never finds out because the relationship will probably end up going nowhere anyway

C) Appreciate the offer, but stay well clear of the person

.

SCENARIO #2: BRIGHT LIGHTS CONT'D

If you answered C, then you're making this light-skinned guru very proud. I'm so proud of you. It takes a considerable amount humbleness and class to turn down such a fine specimen. In this instance, your complexion was used as a filter like on a dating site. However, to your friend, the failure in this endeavor would be severely demoralizing with your friend staring at you, and your complexion at the helm. Trust me, your friend will surely find out the exact reason why the person likes you as oppose to him or her. #itneverfails

But you made the right decision by standing down. You avoided the conflict, drama and stress; keeping your good friends, crew love, and light-skin Christmas morning feeling.

Oh yeah...just totally forget about options A & B and that's being way, way too light-skinned.

NOTES

_____

_____

_____

_____

_____

_____

_____

_____

_____

_____

_____

_____

NOTES

_____

_____

_____

_____

_____

_____

_____

_____

_____

_____

_____

NOTES

NOTES

_____

_____

_____

_____

_____

_____

_____

_____

_____

_____

_____

ABOUT THE AUTHOR

Ron Holloway, a Milwaukee, WI native, resides in the Washington DC metro area where he is a motivational speaker who is changing lives and inspires others to do the same. Ron's books cost less than a latte and are part of the newest literary trend of short books, which make those with short attention spans very happy. More info can be found at iamronholloway.com.

Stay Updated

iamronholloway.com

www.ingramcontent.com/pod-product-compliance
Lightning Source LLC
Chambersburg PA
CBHW070643030426
42337CB00020B/4142